THE SPACE RACE

SPACE STATIONS AND BEYOND

BY
JOHN HAMILTON

Abdo & Daughters
An imprint of Abdo Publishing | abdobooks.com

abdobooks.com

Published by Abdo Publishing, a division of ABDO, PO Box 398166, Minneapolis, Minnesota 55439. Copyright © 2019 by Abdo Consulting Group, Inc. International copyrights reserved in all countries. No part of this book may be reproduced in any form without written permission from the publisher. Abdo & Daughters™ is a trademark and logo of Abdo Publishing.

Printed in the United States of America, North Mankato, Minnesota.
012019
012019

Editor: Sue Hamilton
Copy Editor: Bridget O'Brien
Graphic Design: Sue Hamilton
Cover Design: Candice Keimig and Pakou Moua
Cover Photo: NASA
Interior Images: All images NASA, except Science Source-pg 11; Space Facts-pg 15.

Library of Congress Control Number: 2018949995
Publisher's Cataloging-in-Publication Data
Names: Hamilton, John, author.
Title: Space stations and beyond / by John Hamilton.
Description: Minneapolis, Minnesota : Abdo Publishing, 2019 | Series: The space race | Includes online resources and index.
Identifiers: ISBN 9781532118340 (lib. bdg.) | ISBN 9781532171598 (ebook)
Subjects: LCSH: Space stations--Juvenile literature. | Manned space stations--Juvenile literature. | Space laboratories--Juvenile literature. | Space race--Juvenile literature.
Classification: DDC 629.4--dc23

CONTENTS

Beyond the Space Race 4
Salyut Space Stations 10
Soyuz Spacecraft 12
Soyuz 11 Tragedy 14
Skylab 16
Apollo-Soyuz Test Project 20
Space Shuttle 24
The *Challenger* and *Columbia* Tragedies 28
Mir Space Station 30
International Space Station 34
Future Space Stations 42
Timeline 44
Glossary 46
Online Resources 47
Index 48

BEYOND THE SPACE RACE

On July 20, 1969, astronaut Neil Armstrong, commander of the American Apollo 11 mission, stepped on the Moon. At that moment, the Space Race came to an unofficial end.

During the 1950s and 1960s, the United States and the Soviet Union invested much effort in the race to the Moon. Billions of dollars were spent. Lives were lost. The winner could claim national honor and prestige. Also at stake: learning how to lob bigger and more destructive bombs at each other's cities. The Space Race, after all, was greatly funded or supported by each country's military.

More Moon missions followed Apollo 11. However, public support for manned spaceflight shrank. Planners in the United States and the Soviet Union started thinking about the future. What kind of spacecraft should be built next? The answer: space stations.

The United States space shuttle *Atlantis* and the Russian Mir space station are photographed from a Soyuz spacecraft on July 4, 1995. In the years following the Space Race, joint Russian and American activities helped advance scientific knowledge to both countries.

A space station is a spacecraft that stays in orbit around Earth for a long time, sometimes for many years. It is usually occupied by a crew. Some Russian cosmonauts have spent more than a year at one time aboard a space station. (Several cosmonauts and astronauts have spent time on multiple trips totaling more than one year.)

For more than a century, people have dreamed of living in space. There are many tales of science fiction that take place on space stations. Serious scientists have also pushed for a permanent spacecraft in orbit where astronauts can work.

Space stations can be used in many ways. They are often used as laboratories where unique medicines and materials are produced, thanks to the weightless environment.

INTERNATIONAL SPACE STATION
The ISS has a clear view of Earth as it orbits the planet in 2009.

Space stations are also used to observe Earth, including its landforms and weather. Telescopes and other instruments can also be used to get clearer views of the planets and stars, since space stations are so high up they are free from Earth's thick, light-obscuring atmosphere.

Besides science experiments, space stations are excellent places for astronauts to train, possibly for long-duration trips to Mars or other planets. The lessons learned by working in space for long periods of time help scientists develop new technology for future spaceflights.

During the competitive years of the Space Race, both the United States and the Soviet Union learned the basics of building space stations that could orbit Earth. The Soviets—later the Russians, after the collapse of the Soviet Union in 1991—pursued the goal of building space stations first. Russian cosmonauts have been in space almost continuously since 1971.

Once the Apollo program was finished in the early 1970s, the United States considered building large space stations. But they were considered too expensive and complicated. Instead, the National Aeronautics and Space Administration (NASA) spent most of its efforts building a fleet of space shuttles. They were sent into orbit frequently for short periods of time.

Eventually, the two Space Race competitors, the United States and the Russian Federation, agreed to cooperate. They combined their knowledge and built a large space station, together with several other nations. So far, the International Space Station (ISS) has been the most successful space station in history.

ASTRONAUT AND COSMONAUT: A YEAR IN SPACE

NASA astronaut Scott Kelly (left) and Russian cosmonaut Mikhail Kornienko spent a total of 340 days in space aboard the International Space Station. They arrived on March 27, 2015, and landed back on Earth on March 1, 2016. They were sent to study the long-term effects of living in space.

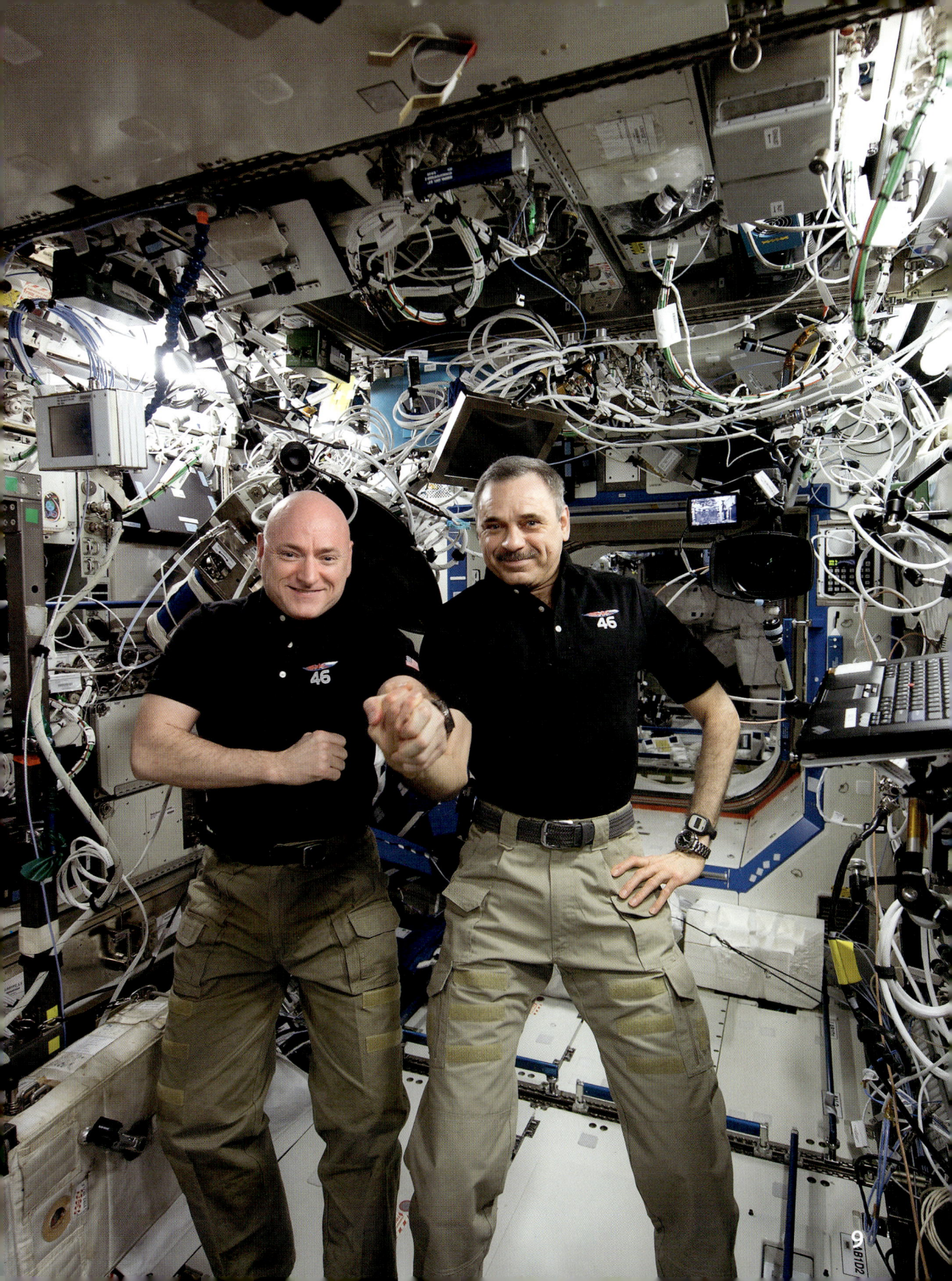

SALYUT SPACE STATIONS

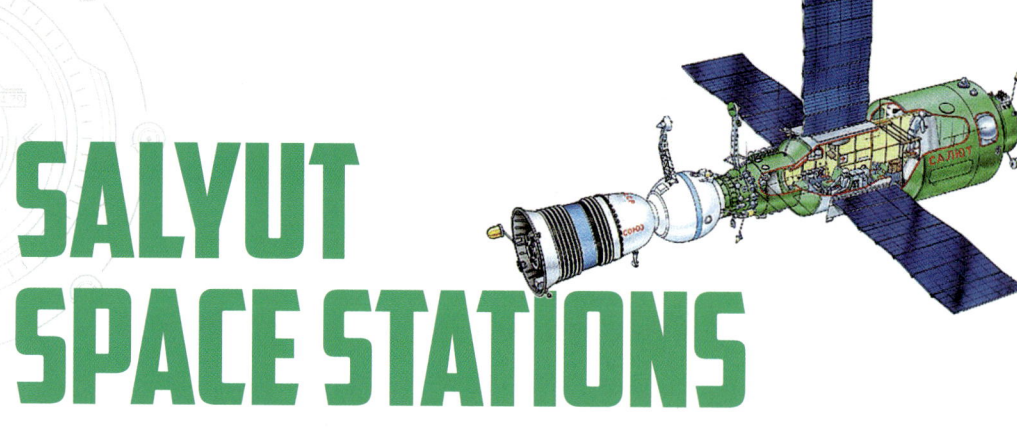

The world's first space station, Salyut 1, was launched into orbit on April 19, 1971, from the Soviet Union's Baikonur Cosmodrome in Kazakhstan. This was a time when America was still sending manned Apollo missions to the Moon.

The Soviets had little hope of equaling the American achievement. Instead, they decided to put more effort into building a permanent presence in space. Salyut 1 was the first in a series of Salyut space stations. (In Russian, the word Salyut means "salute.") Over the next 10 years, 6 more Salyuts followed. Even though 7 Salyuts reached orbit, only six were successfully crewed. (Salyut 2 failed after two days.)

All Salyuts were launched into space in one piece by Proton rockets. Once in orbit, they were powered by two sets of solar panels that jutted outward like wings. Salyut 1 was shaped like a big cylinder, about 66 feet long (20 m) and 13 feet (4 m) in diameter. Later Salyuts were slightly bigger.

The Salyut program was active for about 15 years, until 1986. More than 70 cosmonauts worked on Salyuts for a total of 1,696 days. They entered and left the space stations through a docking port on the end. The cosmonauts conducted experiments and noted how weightlessness affects the human body. Some cosmonauts also conducted secret military experiments. When the Salyut missions were finished, the space stations were allowed to burn up in Earth's atmosphere.

The Salyut 6 space station floats over Earth. Two Soyuz spacecraft are docked on the left and the right ends of the station. The Salyut 6 launched on September 29, 1977, and reentered Earth's atmosphere on July 29, 1982.

11

SOYUZ SPACECRAFT

To carry cosmonauts and supplies to and from space stations, the Russian space program uses the Soyuz spacecraft. (Soyuz means "Union" in Russian.) It has been a workhorse since it was first used by the Soviet Union in 1967 for its Moon program. The spacecraft design has been improved over the years. Today, it is extremely reliable. Soyuz are still flying today to the International Space Station (ISS). They have been used longer than any other manned spacecraft.

Today's Soyuz spacecraft can carry three cosmonauts, plus food, water, and other supplies. The capsule is launched atop a large rocket, which is also called Soyuz. The manned capsule has three parts. They include the orbital, descent, and service modules. The bell-shaped descent module is in the middle. It is the part that returns to Earth.

CLOSE QUARTERS

Expedition 14 astronauts show the close quarters they have in the Soyuz spacecraft. While it takes under 10 minutes to reach space, it is several hours before the craft actually docks with the ISS.

A Soyuz spacecraft is always docked to the ISS. It can act as a lifeboat and emergency escape vehicle in case something happens to the space station and it needs to be evacuated.

Soyuz spacecraft land on the flat, grassy plains of Kazakhstan. They land on the ground because Russia does not keep a large navy at sea at all times to perform rescues. Earth's thick atmosphere slows the spacecraft down. Large parachutes further slow its descent. At the last moment, four retrorockets fire, and the Soyuz lands with a thump. Rescue crews are almost immediately at the scene to help the cosmonauts get out of the spacecraft.

A Soyuz spacecraft lands in Kazakhstan in 2010.

13

SOYUZ 11 TRAGEDY

Soyuz 11 lifts off to dock with Salyut 1, the first space station.

Salyut 1, the Soviet Union's first space station, lifted off on April 19, 1971. When it went into orbit, it did not yet have a crew. Two days later, the Soyuz 10 spacecraft with three cosmonauts aboard blasted off from the Baikonur Cosmodrome on the grassy plains of Kazakhstan. Their mission was supposed to last 30 days, but when they rendezvoused with the space station, they could not get their spacecraft's docking hatch to open to let them inside. The mission was canceled, and they returned to Earth.

On June 6, the Soviets tried again with Soyuz 11 and a new crew. They successfully docked with Salyut 1 and were able to enter the space station. It was the first time in history a space station held a crew. The cosmonauts settled in for a three-week mission that included 383 orbits around Earth. The crew—Georgi Dobrovolski, Vladislav Volkov, and Viktor Patsayev—set a record for the longest time in space.

On June 29, the cosmonauts prepared to go home. They reentered their Soyuz 11 spacecraft and undocked. They were not wearing spacesuits because the capsule was so cramped. They fired their retrorockets and began the long descent to Earth.

Soyuz 11 seemed to reenter the atmosphere and land normally. All systems appeared to be fine, even though controllers on Earth were unable to talk to the cosmonauts on their radio. But when a recovery team opened the capsule, they found all three cosmonauts dead inside, still strapped to their seats.

After an investigation, the Soviets discovered that a ventilation valve had accidentally opened on the Soyuz spacecraft. That decompressed the cabin. The loss of air killed the cosmonauts within minutes. To this day, they are the only three people known to have died in space.

Dobrovolski, Volkov, and Patsayev were hailed as national heroes of the Soviet Union and given state funerals. Afterwards, the Soyuz capsule was modified to only hold two people, which gave the cosmonauts room to wear spacesuits. Soyuz was eventually redesigned and made bigger, allowing three cosmonauts to wear lightweight spacesuits.

The Salyut 1 space station was never used again. On October 11, 1971, orders were given for it to be deorbited. It later broke apart over the Pacific Ocean.

CREW DEATHS

The Soyuz 11 crew (left to right) Viktor Patsayev, Georgi Dobrovolski, and Vladislav Volkov in the cabin of their spacecraft in June 1971. A loss of air in their cabin killed all the men as they returned to Earth.

A modified Saturn V rocket takes Skylab into space on May 14, 1973.

SKYLAB

The United States' first space station was called Skylab. It was a short-term space station where crews performed science experiments in the weightlessness of space.

Skylab was launched on May 14, 1973, a little more than two years after the Soviet Union's Salyut 1 space station. Skylab was boosted into orbit atop a Saturn V rocket. The Saturn V was modified so that its third stage became the orbiting laboratory. Three different crews, of three astronauts each, worked in the space station.

After the Apollo 11 mission to the Moon, NASA recommended future space missions to President Richard Nixon once all the Apollo flights were finished. NASA's ambitious plan included a permanently manned space station. It wanted a fleet of space shuttles to ferry crews and supplies to the space station. Eventually, NASA also wanted to send manned missions to Mars.

Skylab

Because the United States economy was not doing well, only the space shuttle program received full funding from the government. However, after the last two Apollo missions to the Moon were cancelled, NASA decided to use one of the remaining Saturn V rockets to make Skylab affordable. It wanted to prove to the American people that astronauts could live and work in space for long periods of time, and conduct valuable science research.

When Skylab launched in May 1973, it immediately had problems. A micrometeoroid shield tore away and destroyed a solar panel. It also caused another solar panel to stick. The accident meant Skylab had less power than planned. It also caused too much overheating from the Sun without the shield in place.

Skylab's first crew saved the space station with several spacewalks. They managed to replace the heat shield. They also unjammed the stubborn solar panel. Temperatures in Skylab dropped, and the crew was able to work safely inside. The spacewalks and repairs proved the value of having a human crew on future space missions.

Skylab was about 82 feet (25 m) long and 22 feet (7 m) in diameter. It had four major parts. They included an airlock, a docking module, an orbital workshop, and a telescope mount. A solar telescope let the astronauts take pictures of Sun flares.

CLEANING UP

Astronaut Charles Conrad gets a hot shower in Skylab's crew quarters. To use the shower, the curtain pulled up from the floor and attached to the ceiling. The water came through a push button showerhead attached to a flexible hose. Water was drawn off by a vacuum.

18

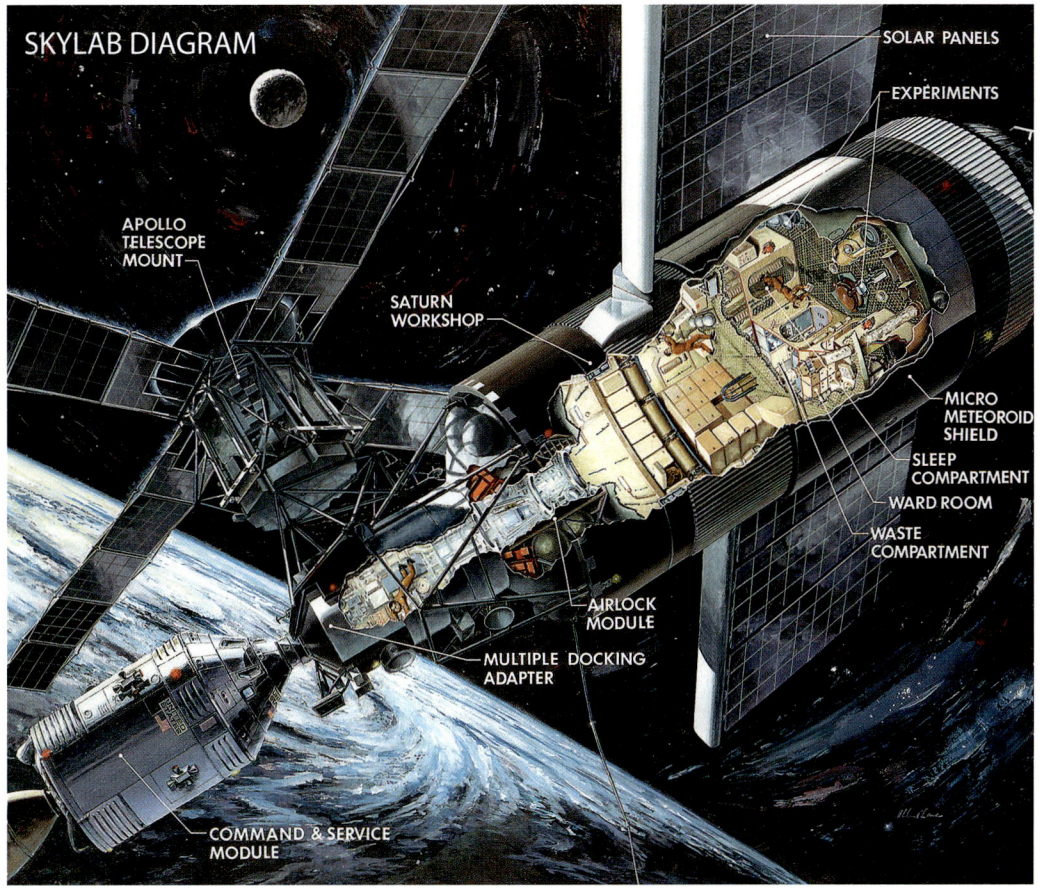

The orbital workshop is where the astronauts worked and slept. NASA tried to make it as comfortable as possible. It had the same amount of room as a small house. It included exercise equipment, private sleeping quarters, a shower, and windows to view Earth.

Skylab was occupied by three different crews, each with three crew members, from May 25, 1973, until February 8, 1974. Together, they performed 270 science experiments in astronomy, physics, and biology. They travelled a total of more than 70 million miles (113 million km) over 171 days in orbit.

When the Skylab program ended, the space station reentered Earth's atmosphere in July 1979. Most of Skylab burned up, but some pieces fell in western Australia. Nobody was injured.

APOLLO-SOYUZ TEST PROJECT

Apollo lifts off with 3 astronauts.

Soyuz lifts off with 2 cosmonauts.

In 1972, the United States and the Soviet Union agreed to fly a space mission together. Three years later, the agreement became reality when the Apollo-Soyuz Test Project launched.

On July 15, 1975, two spacecraft took off from opposite sides of the world. A Soviet Soyuz spacecraft carrying two cosmonauts took off from the Baikonur Cosmodrome in Kazakhstan. A few hours later, three American astronauts atop a Saturn 1B rocket were launched from Kennedy Space Center in Florida. Two days later, the capsules docked together. It was a mission that seemed impossible just a few years earlier.

The Apollo-Soyuz Test Project was the first time that the Space Race rivals worked together on a manned flight. Much work was yet to be done, but the mission was the start of a partnership that eventually saw the construction of the largest space station in history.

On July 17, 1975, a Soviet Soyuz spacecraft (top) docked with an American Apollo spacecraft for the first-ever international space mission.

The Apollo-Soyuz Test Project was designed to see how well Soviet and American spacecraft could dock with each other. The countries realized that in case of a space station emergency, it would be a huge advantage if either side could help the other. But in order for an international rescue mission to work, the docking hardware on all spacecraft had to fit together.

Engineers from the Soviet Union and the United States shared data and experience and designed a new docking module. It fit both the American Apollo spacecraft and the Soviet Soyuz capsule.

The two Soviet cosmonauts on the mission were Alexey Leonov and Valery Kubasov. Leonov was the first person to ever spacewalk. He made history during his Voskhod 2 mission in 1965.

Donald "Deke" Slayton, U.S. Docking Module Pilot

Thomas Stafford, U.S. Crew Commander (Standing)

Vance Brand, U.S. Command Module Pilot

Alexey Leonov, Soviet Crew Commander (Standing)

Valery Kubasov, Soviet Engineer

"GLAD TO SEE YOU." American astronaut Thomas Stafford meets Soviet cosmonaut Alexey Leonov in the hatchway leading from the Apollo docking module to the Soyuz orbital module during the first joint space mission in 1975.

The three American astronauts included Thomas Stafford, Donald "Deke" Slayton, and Vance Brand. Slayton was one of the original Mercury 7 astronauts. He had been grounded because of an irregular heartbeat. The condition had cleared, and Slayton now finally had his chance to go into space.

The two spacecraft met on July 17, 1975. They inched closer together, and then the astronauts felt a slight jolt. They had docked. Soon, the hatches on each capsule opened and commanders Stafford and Leonov shook hands. "Glad to see you," Stafford said in Russian. Leonov smiled and replied in English, "Glad to see you. Very, very happy to see you."

Over the next two days, the astronauts and cosmonauts visited each other's spacecraft and conducted science experiments. They ate meals together and exchanged gifts.

People in both the United States and the Soviet Union were relieved when the joint spaceflight happened. It seemed as if the Cold War was finally starting to thaw. Perhaps the future held more cooperation between the superpowers instead of the constant threat of war.

SPACE SHUTTLE

NASA's space shuttle was the world's first reusable spacecraft. It took off like a rocket, but landed like a glider. It carried heavy payloads, like satellites and science labs, and brought them back to Earth for repair when needed.

The space shuttle was meant to be a cheaper alternative to expensive single-use rockets. It could safely land, be refurbished and refueled, and be ready to launch again in just a few weeks.

The space shuttle had many purposes. It carried astronauts to space stations, and it launched space probes and observatories like the Hubble Space Telescope. It was also used to conduct scientific research on orbital trips that lasted one to two weeks. One of its most important jobs was to launch large parts that were used to build the International Space Station.

REUSABLE SPACECRAFT

Space shuttle *Atlantis* soared into space with a crew of seven and a payload of scientific equipment headed for the ISS in 1992. NASA's space shuttles were used over and over again from the first shuttle flight in 1981 until they were retired in 2011. After 135 shuttle missions over more than 30 years, *Atlantis* made the final flight in July 2011.

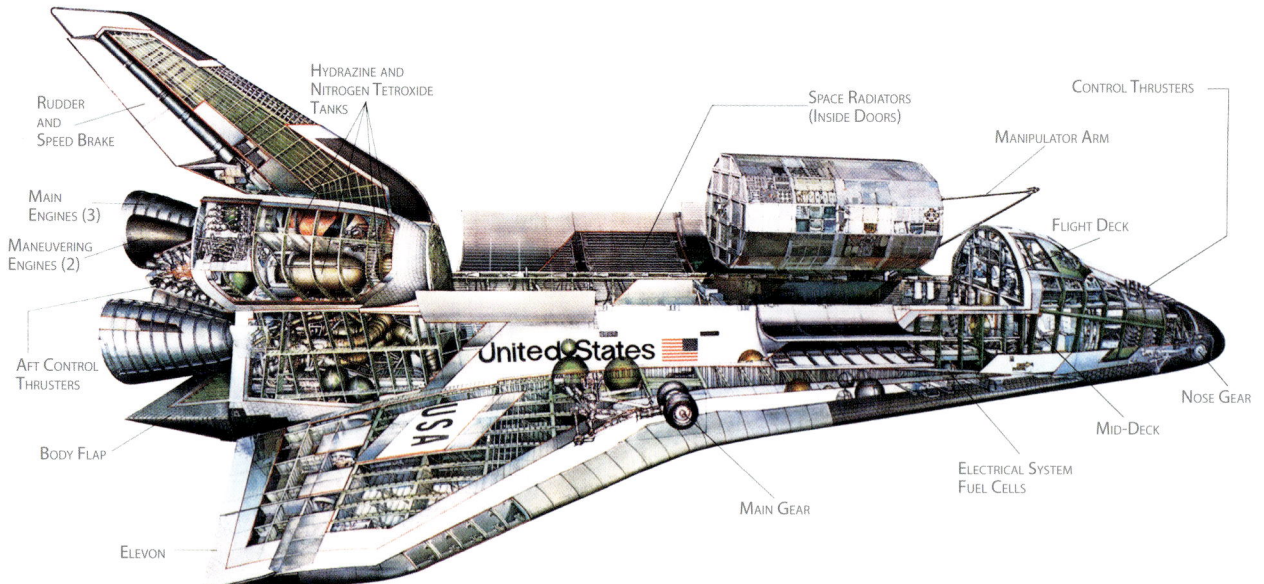

SPACE SHUTTLE DIAGRAM

A cutaway diagram shows the inner workings of a space shuttle orbiter. The huge payload bay transported thousands of pounds of cargo into space.

    The space shuttle was officially called the Space Transportation System. It launched upright, like a rocket. When ready to launch, it was made of three main parts. The orbiter held the crew (usually up to seven astronauts), plus any payload inside its large rear cargo hold. The orbiter measured 122 feet (37 m) long, with a wingspan of 78 feet (24 m). Once in space, the shuttle orbited the Earth at about 17,500 miles per hour (28,164 kph), circling the planet about every 45 minutes.

    Attached to the orbiter at launch was a rust-colored external tank. It supplied 500,000 gallons (1.9 million liters) of liquid oxygen and liquid hydrogen fuel to the orbiter's three main engines. When it ran out of fuel, it ejected from the orbiter. Most of the external tank burned up in the atmosphere.

Two solid-rocket boosters were attached to either side of the external tank. They gave most of the thrust when lifting off. When they ran out of fuel, they dropped off and were picked up in the ocean, to be used by later shuttle flights.

The space shuttle was the size of a modern jetliner, and shaped like an aerodynamic wing (called a delta wing). Its shape allowed it to return to Earth like a glider. Special heat-resistant tiles on its lower half kept it from burning up when reentering the atmosphere. When it descended close to the ground, it lowered its wheels and landed on a runway like an airplane (except for a large parachute it released to help it slow down).

NASA built five fully functioning space shuttle orbiters. They were named *Atlantis, Challenger, Columbia, Discovery,* and *Endeavour*. The first space shuttle flight was in 1981. The final flight occurred in 2011. During this period, there were 135 missions. All flights launched from the Kennedy Space Center in Florida.

Space shuttle *Endeavour* lands at Edwards Air Force Base in California in 2001. The shuttle's large drag chute helped slow the spacecraft on the runway.

THE CHALLENGER AND COLUMBIA TRAGEDIES

By 1986, space shuttle flights were so common they seemed routine. NASA appeared to have perfected spaceflight. On January 28, 1986, that thought was proven tragically wrong.

The space shuttle *Challenger* was starting its 10th mission. Less than two minutes after liftoff, there was a massive explosion in the sky. All seven astronauts were killed. The crew included Commander Francis Scobee, pilot Michael Smith, Ellison Onizuka, Judith Resnik, Ronald McNair, Christa McAuliffe, and Gregory Jarvis. McAuliffe was part of the Teacher in Space program.

NASA later determined that a faulty rubber O-ring seal on one of the solid rocket boosters had hardened because of cold weather. That allowed burning gas to leak like a blowtorch. The flames struck the neighboring external liquid-fuel tank, causing it to explode.

The crew of space shuttle *Challenger* lost their lives searching for knowledge.

COLUMBIA BRAVE

The crew of space shuttle *Columbia* died when the damaged craft broke up during the return flight in 2003. It was, once again, a tragic reminder of the dangers of space travel.

In 2003, tragedy struck the space shuttle program again. On February 1, 2003, in the final minutes of its mission, *Columbia* broke apart over the skies of Texas. During reentry, a broken heat shield panel on the left wing allowed hot gasses to enter. That led to the shuttle's destruction. All seven astronauts died. They included Commander Rick Husband, pilot William McCool, Kalpana Chawla, David Brown, Laurel Clark, Ilan Ramon, and Michael Anderson.

The *Challenger* and *Columbia* disasters led to changes in space shuttle design to make them safer. They also led to NASA management changes. The disasters reminded people that spaceflight is very far from routine. There is always danger when venturing into space.

MIR SPACE STATION

After the success of the Soviet Union's seven Salyut space stations, the Soviets began to build a space station that was much bigger and could be lived in for long periods of time. They named the space station Mir, which means "world" or "peace" in Russian.

Mir was the first modular space station. It was built over time using several large pieces assembled together. The first piece was launched into orbit by a Soviet Proton rocket in 1986. The module had six docking ports for future sections or for visiting spacecraft. Construction on Mir continued until 1996. By then, it had become the largest space station ever built. Mir stayed in orbit 15 years. That was three times longer than expected. It even lasted longer than the Soviet Union. In 1991, control of Mir was transferred to the Russian Federation and its new space agency.

TEN YEARS OF CONSTRUCTION

Mir's first base block (core) module was placed in orbit on February 20, 1986. From then until 1996, modules were added piece by piece to create the huge space station.

When it was completed, Mir had the appearance of a Tinkertoy in space. Many modules jutted out at strange angles. The central module was a living quarters for the crews. It was a large metal cylinder about 43 feet (13 m) long and 14 feet (4 m) in diameter. Electricity came from solar panels that jutted out of the module like wings.

Other modules were added over the next decade. They included an observatory, science labs, and an additional life-support module. Most of the cosmonauts traveled to and from the space station by Soyuz spacecraft. Supplies were sent by unmanned Progress cargo spacecraft.

Despite its appearance, the station was a success. It proved that people could live in orbit for months at a time. Mir was a science laboratory in space. Besides testing human biology in a weightless environment, the station's crews performed many experiments in botany, physics, astronomy, and biomedicine. They also learned valuable knowledge about spacecraft systems.

CROWDED

Cosmonaut Yury Onofrienko floats through Mir's base block module in 1996. After 10 years, the huge space station was packed with equipment, electronics, computers, cameras, and science experiments.

32

Cosmonaut Valery Polyakov looks out a window in 1994 as space shuttle *Discovery* arrives at Mir.

Mir had 28 different crews during its lifetime. Each mission lasted about six months, but some cosmonauts stayed longer. Valery Polyakov set a space endurance record between January 1994 and March 1995. He lived on the space station for 438 days in a row. Mir's crews were mostly Russian cosmonauts, but the space station also hosted dozens of guests from countries all over the world.

Starting in the mid-1990s, American space shuttles began docking with Mir. American astronauts and equipment were also delivered to the space station. The space shuttle-Mir missions were part of a new cooperation between the space programs of the United States and Russia. The lessons learned would later be used to construct the most ambitious spacecraft in history: the International Space Station.

In March 2001, the Russian space agency used retrorockets on the aging Mir to bring it down to Earth. The deorbit happened over the Pacific Ocean. Most of Mir burned up, but some flaming debris splashed into the ocean.

33

INTERNATIONAL SPACE STATION

The fierce Space Race competition between the Soviet Union—later Russia—and the United States eventually led to cooperation between the two superpower rivals. Each side knew it was best to combine their knowledge—and money—to make a new space station that would be better than either side could make alone. In fact, their plans were so ambitious, many other countries of the world also helped. The result was the International Space Station (ISS).

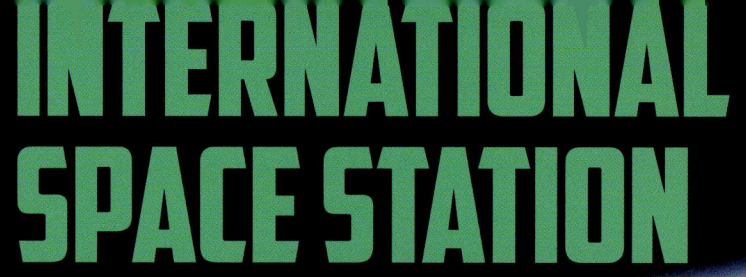

The ISS has been continuously crewed since November 2000. It is a modular space station, like Mir. Large sections are continuously added. It orbits an average of 240 miles (386 km) above Earth. It takes about 90 minutes to complete one orbit around the planet.

Today, the ISS is an orbiting science laboratory. The crew of astronauts are learning the best ways to live and work in space. This information will help future astronauts explore distant places in our solar system, perhaps even Mars.

International Space Station Assembly

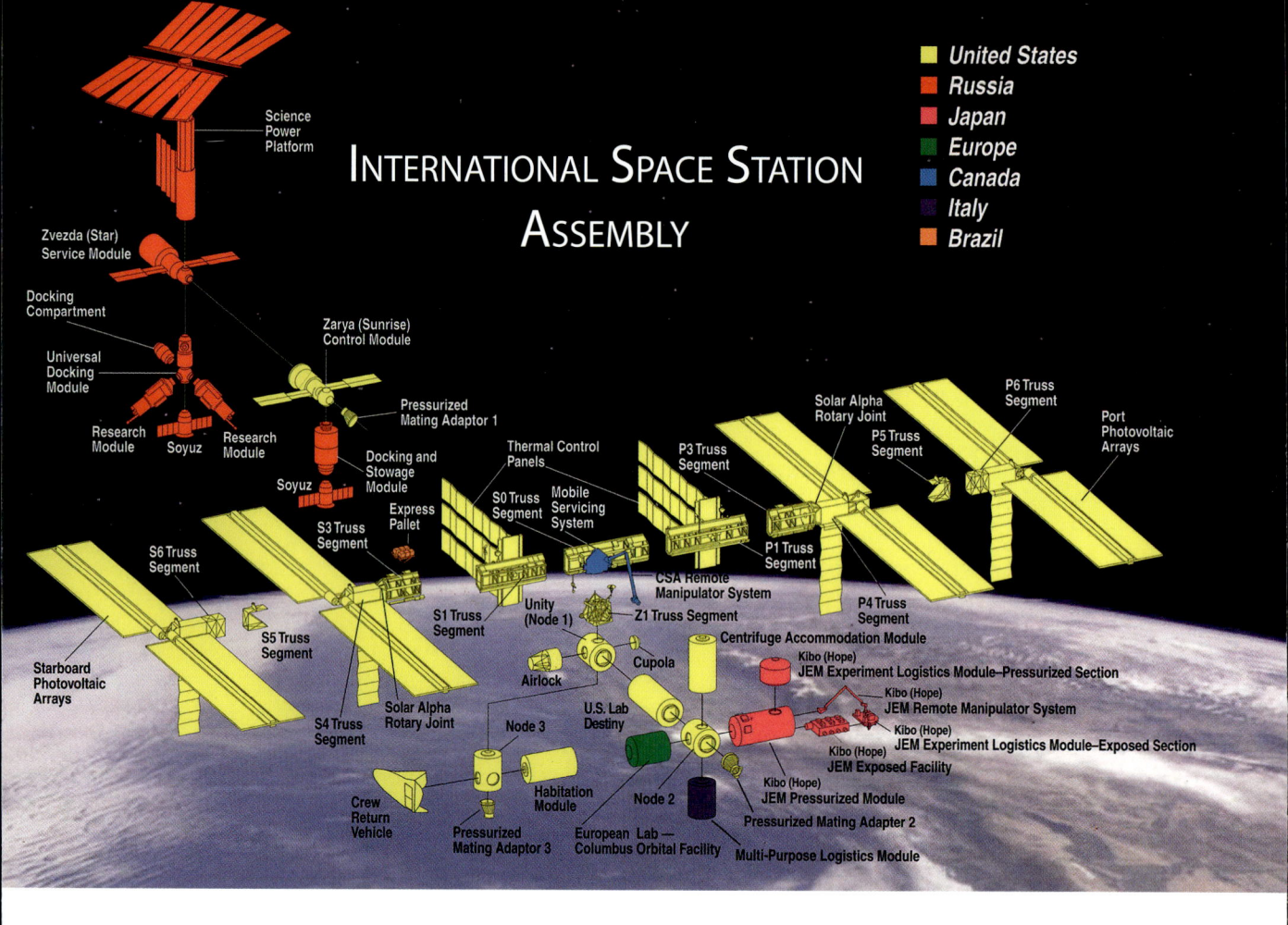

Construction of the ISS took years to plan and the help of 15 nations. The station's five main partners include NASA and space agencies from Russia, Europe, Canada, and Japan. Russia launched the first piece of the ISS, called Zarya, into orbit in 1998. A few weeks later, an American module called Unity was connected. Dozens of modules have been added in the years since.

ISS Insignia

Additional modules were brought to the ISS by Russian rockets and NASA's fleet of space shuttles. It took more than 115 space flights to bring all the pieces needed to construct the space station, at a cost of about $100 billion.

The first two pieces of the ISS were the Soviet's Zarya and the American's Unity, which were joined together in 1998.

The first ISS crew.

Sergei Krikalev, Soviet Flight Engineer 2

William Shepherd, U.S. Commander

Yuri Gidzenko, Soviet Flight Engineer 1

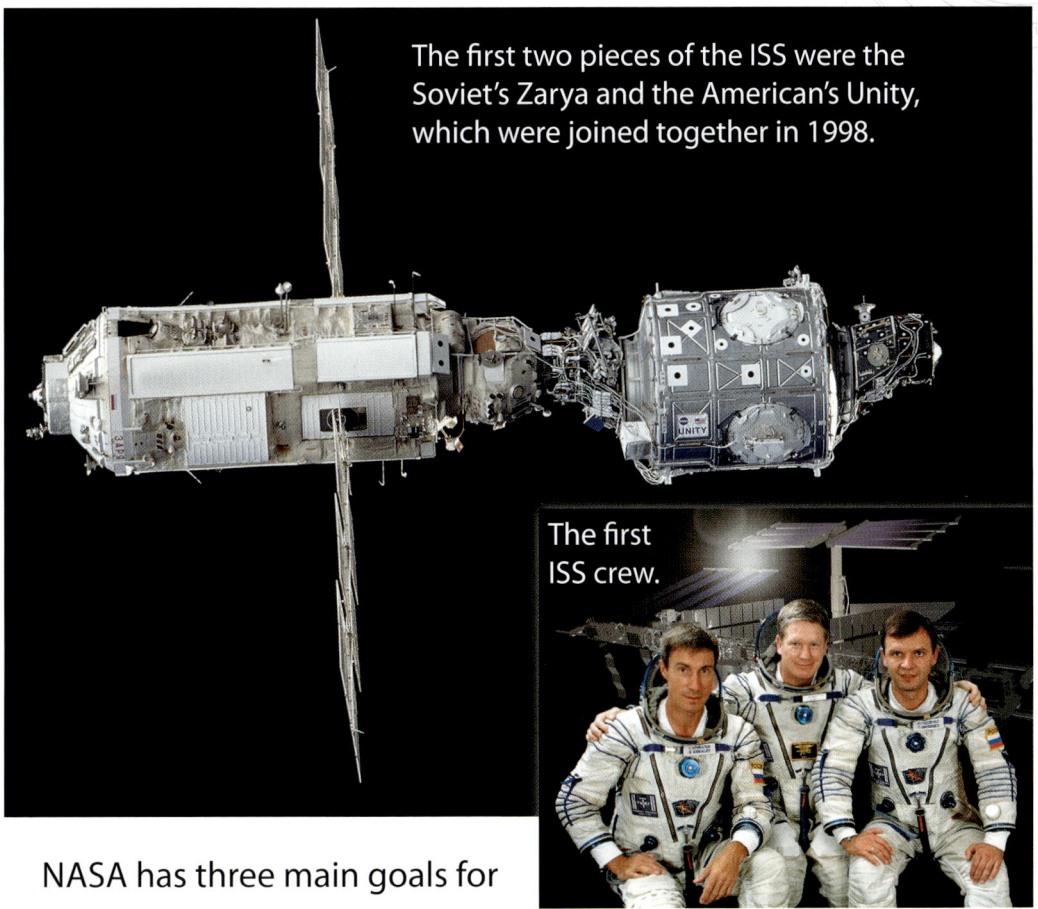

NASA has three main goals for the ISS. It is a place for astronauts to conduct scientific research in a weightless environment. It establishes a constant, long-term presence in space. It also encourages many countries to work together.

Fully crewed, the ISS can support six astronauts. The first long-term crew to live aboard the ISS arrived in 2000. They included Sergei Krikalev and Yuri Gidzenko from Russia, and William Shepherd of the United States. Astronauts have lived on the ISS ever since that date.

Over its lifetime, crews from many nations have lived on the ISS. They have added additional living quarters, science laboratories, solar panels, and communications systems.

37

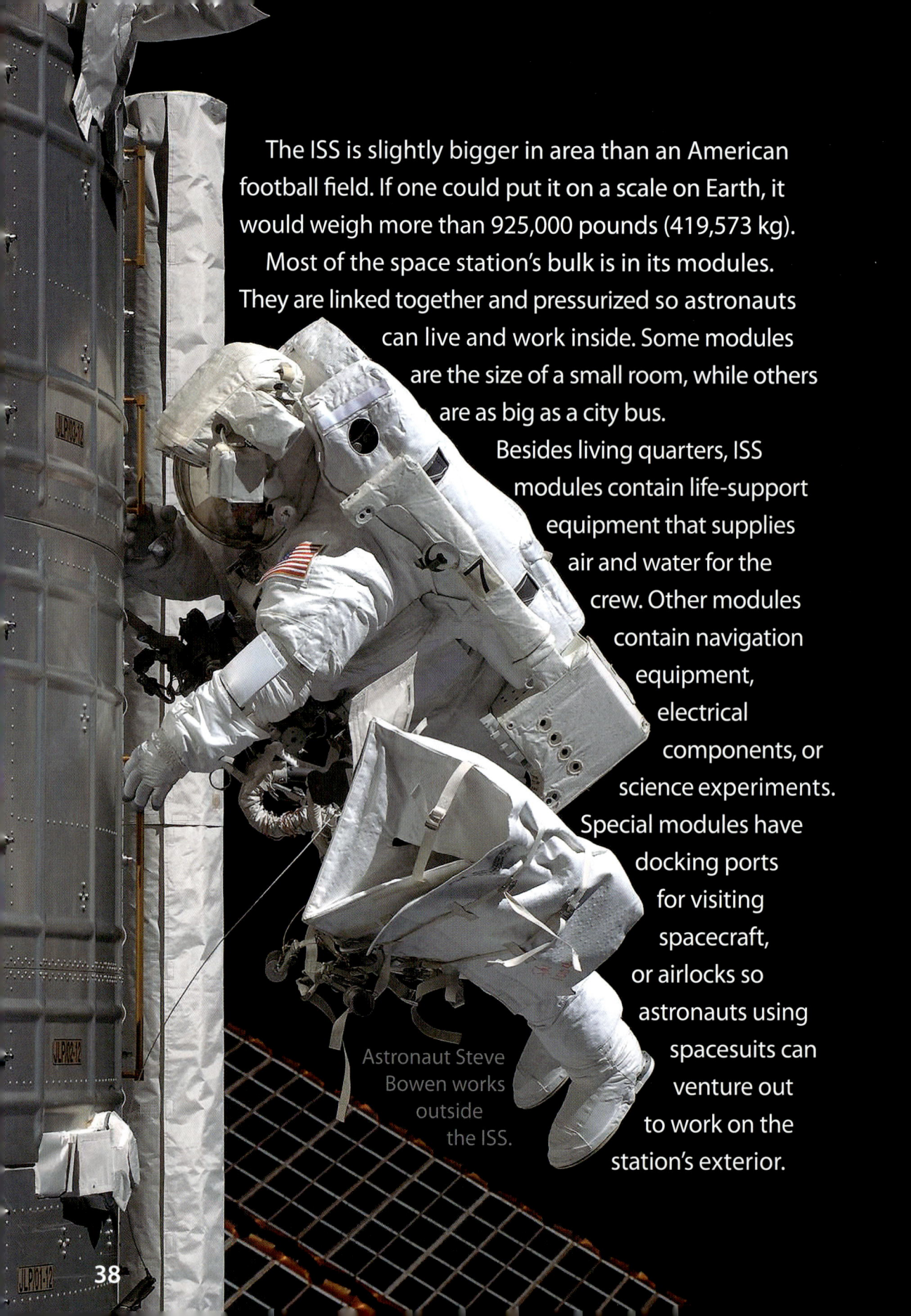

The ISS is slightly bigger in area than an American football field. If one could put it on a scale on Earth, it would weigh more than 925,000 pounds (419,573 kg). Most of the space station's bulk is in its modules. They are linked together and pressurized so astronauts can live and work inside. Some modules are the size of a small room, while others are as big as a city bus.

Besides living quarters, ISS modules contain life-support equipment that supplies air and water for the crew. Other modules contain navigation equipment, electrical components, or science experiments. Special modules have docking ports for visiting spacecraft, or airlocks so astronauts using spacesuits can venture out to work on the station's exterior.

Astronaut Steve Bowen works outside the ISS.

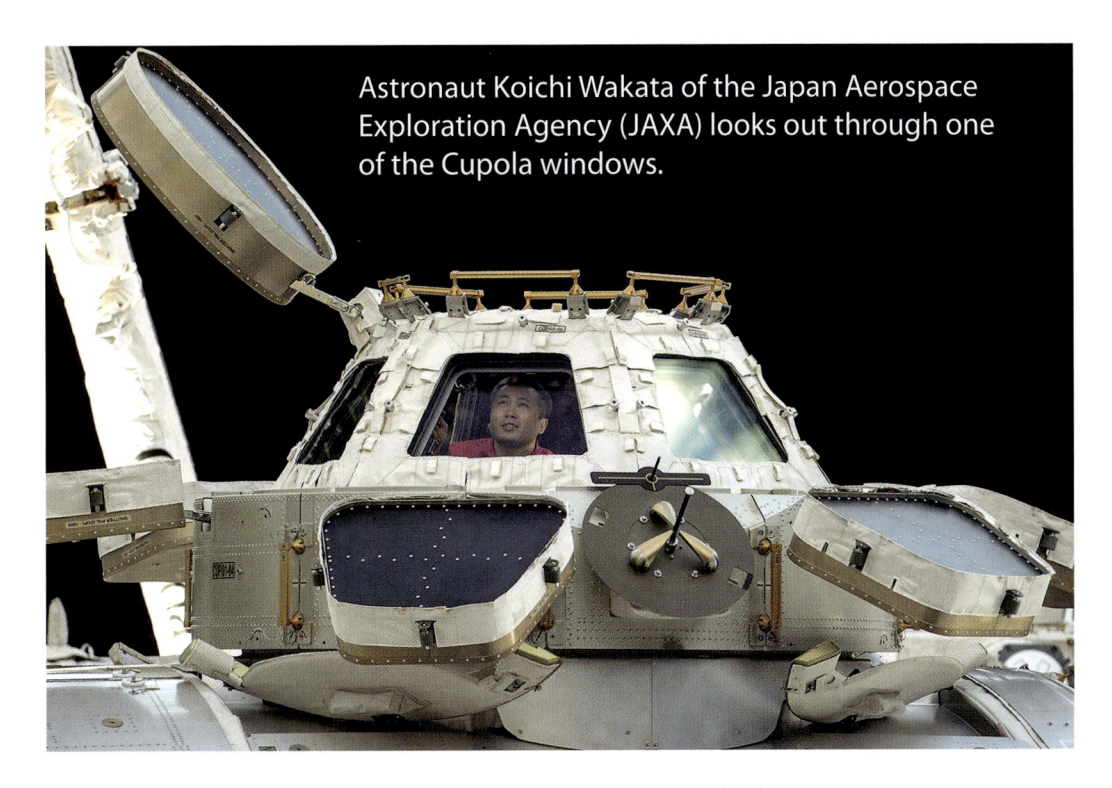

Astronaut Koichi Wakata of the Japan Aerospace Exploration Agency (JAXA) looks out through one of the Cupola windows.

One special module is the Cupola. Built in Italy, the dome-shaped Cupola has large windows that give astronauts a panoramic view of the space station and the Earth. The windows are useful when astronauts use the ISS's Canadarm2 robotic arm system. Made in Canada, it is used to assemble and repair the outside of ISS modules. It can also capture and dock unmanned supply spacecraft that visit the ISS.

The ISS gets its electrical power from large solar arrays. They are made of thousands of solar cells that absorb energy from the Sun and convert it into electricity. The solar arrays are arranged in four pairs on each side of the space station. Each array is about 240 feet (73 m) long, which is longer than the wingspan of a Boeing 777 airliner. When the ISS moves into Earth's shadow during its 90-minute orbit, the space station gets its power from rechargeable batteries.

Sleep Cubby

Food

Treadmill

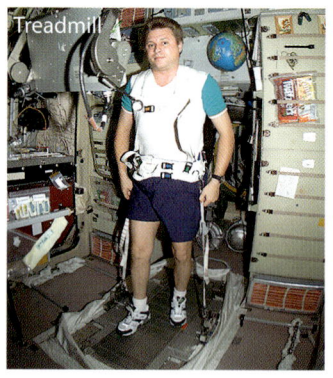

Toilet

There are usually three to six people living aboard the ISS at once. Astronauts and cosmonauts from 17 different countries have lived and worked on the space station. ISS missions are called expeditions. Each usually lasts about 6 months.

Living on the ISS is much more comfortable than earlier space stations. Astronauts sleep inside their own closet-sized cubbies. Sleeping bags provide warmth and keep the astronauts from floating away. After waking, they wash with moist towels. There are no showers because water bubbles might float into electronic equipment and cause damage.

Most food aboard the ISS is dehydrated to save space. Water is first added before eating. Astronauts drink water that comes in a package with a straw on the end.

Exercise is important so that astronauts don't lose too much bone density and muscle mass while in orbit. They stay in shape using a treadmill, stationary bike, and weight-lifting machine.

The ISS toilet is a small booth. Crew members pee into a vacuum tube that whisks away urine. Poop is disposed of by sitting on a small metal seat with a hole on top. A vacuum sucks away any solid waste. Accidental messes are cleaned up with disinfectant wipes.

Astronaut Karen Nyberg works in the Kibo laboratory of the ISS.

Astronauts stay very busy on the ISS. The space station is used to conduct many science experiments. Many chemistry, physics, and biology experiments can only be carried out in the weightlessness of space. The Japanese Kibo space laboratory is the single largest module on the ISS. It is used to conduct research in astronomy, biology, and space medicine. It is possible that someday many medicines and special materials will be manufactured in space, thanks to the research done on the ISS. There are even plans to grow human hearts and other organs in space.

Eventually, the ISS will be too old to maintain and will have to be replaced. For now, NASA expects the space station to operate at least until the 2020s and possibly a decade or two beyond. When the ISS finally reaches the end of its lifespan, it will be remotely steered out of orbit. Most of it will burn up in Earth's atmosphere, although some large pieces of debris may survive and fall into uninhabited areas, such as the Pacific Ocean.

FUTURE SPACE STATIONS

The International Space Station (ISS) is not the only space station currently in orbit around Earth. In 2011, China launched a small space station called Tiangong-1. It was followed by Tiangong-2 in 2016. Tiangong-1's orbit eventually decayed. It may have burned up in Earth's atmosphere in early 2018. A larger modular Chinese space station is planned to be put in orbit by 2022. It will be about one-fifth the size of the ISS.

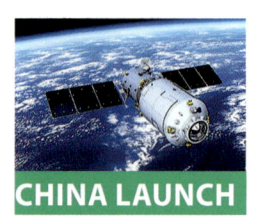

CHINA LAUNCH
China launched their own space stations Tiangong-1 in 2011 and Tiangong-2 in 2016.

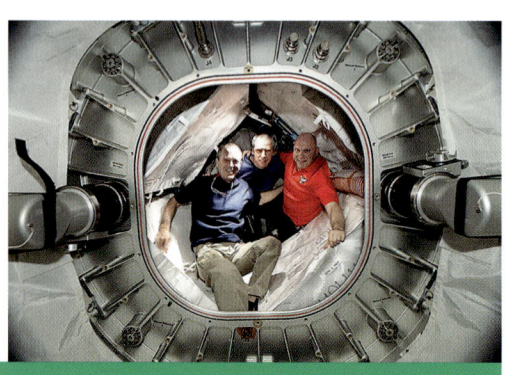

Besides whole nations, private companies are also making plans to put small space stations in orbit. Genesis 1 and Genesis 2 are experimental unmanned space stations launched in 2006 and 2007 by an American company called Bigelow Aerospace. The stations use inflatable modules that are lighter to launch and provide more interior room than regular rigid modules.

BEAM
Astronauts Ricky Arnold and Drew Feustel and cosmonaut Oleg Artemyev float inside the Bigelow Expandable Aerospace Module (BEAM). BEAM was installed on the International Space Station's Tranquility module on April 16, 2016.

LUNAR ORBITAL PLATFORM GATEWAY

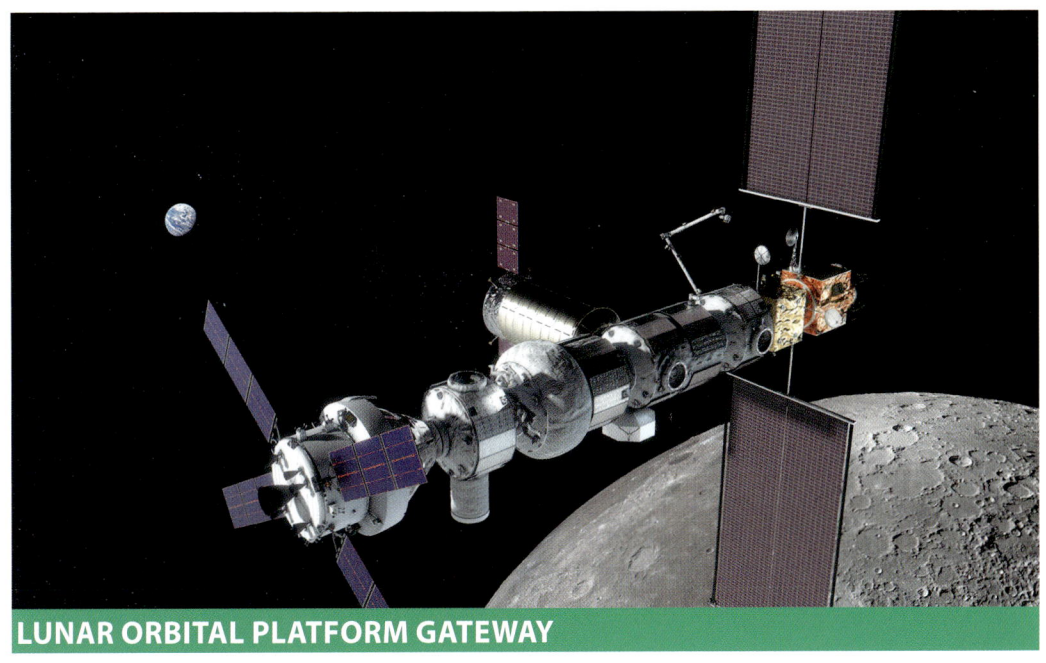

NASA's Lunar Orbital Platform Gateway (LOP-G) space station is scheduled to launch sometime in the mid-2020s. It will be in cislunar space between the Earth and the Moon. LOP-G will be supplied by the new Orion spacecraft.

Orbiting Earth isn't the only place for space stations. NASA is now planning and designing the Lunar Orbital Platform Gateway (LOP-G). It is a mini version of the ISS. It will operate in cislunar space, between Earth and the Moon. It will be constructed sometime in the mid-2020s by astronauts flying in NASA's new Orion spacecraft and Space Launch System (SLS) rocket.

LOP-G is designed to teach scientists how astronauts can best work and live in deep space, thousands of times farther from Earth than the ISS. Astronauts aboard LOP-G will also be able to perform science experiments, and possibly control robots on the Moon.

If all goes well with the LOP-G project, it may even be used as a supply station to construct and fly future spacecraft that will take astronauts to Mars and beyond.

TIMELINE

1957, October 4—The Soviet Union launches the Sputnik 1 satellite. It marks the unofficial start of the Space Race.

1967, April 23—First launch of a Soyuz spacecraft with a crew.

1971, April 19—The Soviet Union's Salyut 1 space station is launched into orbit. It is the world's first space station.

1971, July 29—The crew of Soyuz 11 reenters Earth's atmosphere after a successful three-week mission aboard the Salyut space station. Tragically, a faulty valve on the spacecraft opened and caused the crew cabin to depressurize. All three Soviet cosmonauts were killed.

1971, October 11—Salyut 1 deorbits and burns up in Earth's atmosphere.

1973, May 14—America's first space station, Skylab, is launched into orbit around Earth.

1975, July 15—The Apollo-Soyuz Test Project is launched, a joint mission between the United States and the Soviet Union. One spacecraft from each country meet on July 17 and stay docked for two days.

1979, July—Skylab deorbits and burns up in Earth's atmosphere.

1981, April 12—Space shuttle *Columbia* launches, the first orbital flight of an American space shuttle.

1991, December 25—The Soviet Union collapses. Part of the country becomes the Russian Federation, commonly known today simply as Russia. The Mir space station comes under the control of Russia.

1986, January 28—Space shuttle *Challenger* explodes shortly after launch, killing all seven astronauts aboard.

1986, February 20—First module of the Soviet Union's Mir space station goes into orbit.

1994–1995—Soviet cosmonaut Valery Polyakov sets a space endurance record of 438 consecutive days aboard the Mir space station.

1998, November 20—The first piece of the International Space Station, the Russian module Zarya, is launched into orbit.

1998, December 6—The first American module of the International Space Station, Unity, is attached to the Soviet module Zarya. First connection between two modules of the space station.

2001, March 23—Mir space station is deorbited. It burns up and disintegrates over the Pacific Ocean.

2003, February 1—Space shuttle *Columbia* disintegrates shortly before landing, killing all seven astronauts aboard.

2006, July 12—American company Bigelow Aerospace launches Genesis 1 unmanned experimental space habitat.

2011, July 8—Space shuttle *Atlantis* launches, the last flight of an American space shuttle.

2011, September 29—Chinese Tiangong-1 space station is launched.

2020s—NASA's Lunar Orbital Platform Gateway plans to launch and enter cislunar space between Earth and the Moon.

GLOSSARY

Astronaut
Someone who travels in a spacecraft. The word has Greek roots that stand for "star sailor" or "star traveller."

Canadarm
The Canadarm and Canadarm2 robotic arm systems were developed and made in Canada. Canadarm was used on the space shuttle. Canadarm2 is currently used on the International Space Station (ISS) to help assemble and repair ISS modules. It can also capture and dock unmanned supply spacecraft.

Cold War
The Cold War was a time of political, economic, and cultural tension between the United States and its allies and the Soviet Union and other Communist nations. It lasted from about 1947, just after the end of World War II, until the early 1990s, when the Soviet Union collapsed and Communism was no longer a major threat to the United States.

Cosmonaut
An astronaut from Russia or the former Soviet Union.

Cupola
A dome-shaped module on the ISS. It is attached to the larger Tranquility module. It was built in Italy and attached to the ISS in 2010. Its large windows give astronauts a panoramic view of the Earth. The circular central window is 31.5 inches (80 cm) in diameter, the largest window ever used in space.

National Aeronautics and Space Administration (NASA)
A United States government space agency started in 1958. NASA's goals include space exploration and increasing people's understanding of Earth, our solar system, and the universe.

Orbit
The path a moon or spacecraft makes when traveling around a planet or other large celestial body. The International Space Station takes about 90 minutes to make one complete orbit around the Earth.

Rendezvous
A meeting at a specific time and place.

Soviet Union
A former country that included a union of Russia and several other Communist republics. It was formed in 1922 and existed until 1991.

Space Shuttle
American's first reusable space vehicle. NASA built five orbiters: *Columbia*, *Challenger*, *Atlantis*, *Discovery*, and *Endeavour*. Two shuttles and their crews were destroyed by accidents: *Challenger* in 1986, and *Columbia* in 2003.

ONLINE RESOURCES

Booklinks NONFICTION NETWORK
FREE! ONLINE NONFICTION RESOURCES

To learn more about space stations and beyond, visit **abdobooklinks.com** or scan this QR code. These links are routinely monitored and updated to provide the most current information available.

INDEX

A
America (*see* United States)
Anderson, Michael 29
Apollo (program) 8, 10, 18, 22
Apollo 11 4, 16
Apollo-Soyuz Test Project 20, 22
Armstrong, Neil 4
Atlantis 27
Australia 19

B
Baikonur Cosmodrome 10, 14, 20
Bigelow Aerospace 42
Boeing 777 39
Brand, Vance 23
Brown, David 29

C
Canada 36, 39
Canadarm2 39
Challenger 27, 28, 29
Chawla, Kalpana 29
China 41
Clark, Laurel 29
Cold War 23
Columbia 27, 29
Cupola 39

D
Discovery 27
Dobrovolski, Georgi 14, 15

E
Earth 6, 7, 8, 10, 12, 13, 14, 15, 19, 24, 26, 27, 33, 35, 38, 39, 41, 42, 43
Endeavour 27
Europe 36

F
Florida 20, 27

G
Genesis 1 42
Genesis 2 42
Gidzenko, Yuri 37

H
Hubble Space Telescope 24
Husband, Rick 29

I
International Space Station (*see* ISS)
ISS 8, 12, 13, 24, 33, 34, 35, 36, 37, 38, 39, 40, 41, 42, 43
Italy 39

J
Japan 36, 41
Jarvis, Gregory 28

K
Kazakhstan 10, 13, 14, 20
Kennedy Space Center 20, 27
Kibo space laboratory 41
Krikalev, Sergei 37
Kubasov, Valery 22

L
Leonov, Alexey 22, 23
Lunar Orbital Platform Gateway (LOP-G) 43

M
Mars 7, 16, 35, 43
McAuliffe, Christa 28
McCool, William 29
McNair, Ronald 28
Mercury 7 23
Mir 30, 32, 33, 35
Moon 4, 10, 12, 16, 18, 43

N
NASA 8, 16, 18, 19, 24, 27, 28, 29, 36, 37, 41, 43
National Aeronautics and Space Administration (*see* NASA)
Nixon, Richard 16

O
Onizuka, Ellison 28
Orion 43

P
Pacific Ocean 15, 33, 41
Patsayev, Viktor 14, 15
Polyakov, Valery 33
Progress cargo spacecraft 32
Proton rocket 10, 30

R
Ramon, Ilan 29
Resnik, Judith 28
Russia (*see* Russian Federation)
Russian Federation 8, 13, 30, 33, 34, 36, 37

S
Salyut (space stations) 10, 30
Salyut 1 10, 14, 15, 16
Salyut 2 10
Saturn 1B 20
Saturn V 16, 18
Scobee, Francis 28
Shepherd, William 37
Skylab 16, 18, 19
Slayton, Donald "Deke" 23
Smith, Michael 28
Soviet Union 4, 8, 10, 12, 14, 15, 16, 20, 22, 23, 30, 34
Soyuz (rocket) 12
Soyuz (spacecraft) 12, 13, 15, 20, 22, 32
Soyuz 10 14
Soyuz 11 14, 15
Space Launch System (SLS) rocket 43
Space Race 4, 8, 20, 34
space shuttle-Mir missions 33
Space Transportation System 26
Stafford, Thomas 23
Sun 18, 39

T
Teacher in Space 28
Texas 29
Tiangong-1 42
Tiangong-2 42

U
United States 4, 8, 10, 16, 18, 20, 22, 23, 33, 34, 37, 42
Unity 36

V
Volkov, Vladislav 14, 15
Voskhod 2 22

Z
Zarya 36

48